Harald Weisshaar

Sir Fox Bones

and the Buckingham Palace Mystery

mit Hör-CD

Ernst Klett Verlag
Stuttgart · Leipzig

1. Auflage 1 8 7 6 | 2016 15

Alle Drucke dieser Auflage sind unverändert und können im Unterricht nebeneinander verwendet werden. Die letzten Zahlen bezeichnen jeweils die Auflage und das Jahr des Druckes.

www.klett.de

Illustrationen: Lars Benecke, Hannover
sowie Christian Dekelver, Weinstadt; Naomi Fearn, Berlin; Uwe Häntsch, Berlin; David Norman, Meerbusch; Sven Palmowski, Barcelona; Steffen Wolff, Düsseldorf; Dorothee Wolters, Köln.
Druck: AZ Druck und Datentechnik GmbH, Kempten
Printed in Germany.
ISBN 978-3-12-547073-6

9 783125 470736

Contents

Before you read

1 The cover

a) What can you see in the picture?

b) What do you think the story is about?
You can find some clues here:

M	D	N	G	J	I	E	W	Q	F
Q	U	E	E	N	J	D	X	D	W
W	Q	B	T	H	B	E	T	I	C
D	O	N	F	E	U	A	F	S	R
G	P	A	L	A	C	E	O	U	G
K	H	U	V	P	K	T	S	B	E
W	A	I	F	H	I	G	I	S	A
D	S	P	O	X	N	H	Z	V	Y
B	H	X	X	B	G	O	Z	G	E
M	E	H	O	C	H	R	E	Y	D
W	Q	H	U	S	A	A	N	M	K
A	X	S	I	I	M	T	E	N	L

detective, Queen, Buckingham, Palace, fox, cat, rat

2 Detectives

a) Do you know any detectives from books or from TV?

b) What is a detective story about?

cover [ˈkʌvə] Buchumschlag • **clue** [klu:] Hinweis

1 The visitor

Ah, there is a noise. Someone is outside my office door. Who can it be? I open the door and look out.

"Sir, can I come in, please?"

Thank God – it is only a dog. He comes in. His tail is very short and his ears are small and round. I do not know him. What can he want?

He looks at me with his big black eyes. "Are you Sir Fox Bones, the famous detective?"

"Well, can't you read what it says on my door?" I tell him and smile. But he looks so sad and tired. So I say, "Sorry! The answer is – yes, I'm Bones … Fox Bones."

"Oh, good, very good, Sir – I need your help," the dog says.

He looks at me again with his big black eyes. Now I see the beautiful collar round his neck. It looks very, very expensive.

He says, "Please don't tell your friends at Foxland Yard about my visit."

Now that is interesting. My visitor has got a job for me – and I like my detective work. So I ask him, "What can I do for you? And who are you?"

He finds it hard to speak, but he tries. "My name is Pharos of Pembroke. I live in Buckingham Palace with the Queen. And this is why I'm here, too."

I think there must be something wrong with my ears. A corgi? One of the Queen's dogs? This is a joke, I think. It must be. But Pharos the dog looks at me and says, "Can I have some water, please? It's a long way to walk from Buckingham Palace to Butcher Road – a long way for a dog with short legs."

1 **noise** [nɔɪz] Geräusch • **someone** ['sʌmwʌn] jemand • **office** ['ɒfɪs] Büro • 8 **bone** [bəʊn] Knochen • 10 **sad** [sæd] traurig • 15 **collar** ['kɒlə] Halsband • **neck** [nek] Hals • 23 **Pharos of Pembroke** [ˌfærɒs‿əv 'pembrʊk] *Name* • 26 **corgi** ['kɔ:gi] *Hunderasse* • 29 **butcher** ['bʊtʃə] Metzger/-in

"I'm sorry, Mr Pharos," is all I can say. "Dr Catson, some water for our visitor," I shout. My assistant Dr Catson comes in with some water.

The dog speaks again, "Oh, hello there. You must be Dr Catson. Nice to meet you. I'm Pharos the corgi – one of the Queen's corgis. But she doesn't know I'm here."

So my ears are OK ... he said it again.

"Ahem – Mr Pharos ... how can we help you? And do you want more water ... or something to eat?" I ask.

"No, thank you," Pharos says. "I haven't got much time."

What a poor dog, I think. He looks so tired. And he looks nervous, too. Again and again, he looks at the door. Why does he do this? Who is after him?

My assistant says, "It's OK – you're safe here." So Catson can see that Pharos is nervous, too. I think about his words again. What does he mean, 'safe'? London is a big place – how can you be safe in London? There are so many animals, and some work for bad people. When we talk to Pharos, we do not know that other animals know he is in my house ... dangerous animals. Later, I will smell danger – but not now. I am very cool.

I tell him, "Now try and tell us what the problem is, and then I think we can help you."

I look at the dog and his collar again. What he says must be true. So he really comes from Buckingham Palace – all the way to talk to me and my assistant. A long way for such a small dog. That is interesting – very, very interesting.

Find the way from Buckingham Palace to Butcher Road on the map on pages 30 and 31. You can take the Underground, too.

7 said [sed] sagte • **12 poor** [pʊə] arm, bedauernswürdig • **15 safe** [seɪf] sicher • **21 will** [wɪl] werde • **to smell** [smel] riechen • **31 Underground** ['ʌndəgraʊnd] U-Bahn

2 The job

So Pharos tells us his story. It is a very long story, and it is interesting:

People must not know he is here. The Queen does not know he is here. She is very, very sad, but she does not tell anybody because she thinks it is dangerous when people hear how easy it is to take things from Buckingham Palace. Her things, her private things.

STOP Why do you think the Queen is so sad?

We don't understand how this can happen: Buckingham Palace is full of cameras. No-one can come and go. And nobody can take the Queen's things. They cannot get them out of the Palace – or can they? And what are these things?

"The Queen doesn't know what to do," Pharos says, "you know, spoons are missing. The spoons are very old and special to her. They are from her grandma. That's why she's so sad."

"The Queen really doesn't know what to do," Pharos says. "Can you and Dr Catson come to the Palace and find the thief?"

What thief? And how can we get into the Palace – it is OK for a cat, but a fox? Yes, I know, a fox is a clever animal, and I am a very clever fox, a master detective. But what do you think – all the cameras in Buckingham Palace, all the policemen, aren't they too dangerous for me?

---

10 **no-one** ['nəʊwʌn] niemand • **to get out** [get 'aʊt] herausbringen • 15 **spoon** [spu:n] Löffel • **are missing** ['mɪsɪŋ] fehlen • 20 **thief** [θi:f] Dieb/-in

Who can you see in the picture? Who is listening to the story? Find more clues in the story.

Someone is listening to Pharos's story. But he cannot hear everything.

Queen • expensive spoons • an old cupboard in the State Dining Room • only one door into the room • every day the Queen • count • only she • key • open the cupboard • who? • and how?

Tell the full story in your own words.

I have a quick word with my assistant, and then I speak to Pharos again. "OK," I say, "we think we can help you. But there are some problems. Problem number one: You must help us to get inside Buckingham Palace. Problem number two: We must stay in the Palace and watch the room ... one night, two nights ... and problem number three: The Queen doesn't know you are here, so who can give us some money for our work?"

Dr Catson looks at me. He thinks I am very clever. He likes it when I am clever like this. For a second, Pharos does not say anything. But then his mouth opens and his pink tongue comes out. "Sir Fox, Dr Catson – we've got friends in London, and we've got friends in Buckingham Palace. They can help us, of course. When you're inside, we can show you where the State Dining Room is. And we can show you where you can sit and watch. One night, two nights, or four weeks! No problem! There is a lot of good food for animals in the Palace, so that's OK, too."

Pharos thinks for a minute, and then he says, "You're right – the Queen doesn't know I'm here, and she doesn't know that you can come to the Palace and help us. But I know that you can find the thief. It's easy: You catch the thief, we tell the Queen. Then she can be happy and safe again. So she gives you money, or ... other things."

Dr Catson and I like the plan. But let's think again about what Pharos said. "We've got friends in London." Yes, it is true, he has got friends in London. But I feel that he has got enemies, too, these animals do not like Pharos.

Pharos says goodbye to my assistant and me. It is the last time we see the Queen's corgi.

He says, "Meet me outside Buckingham Palace at 11.30 am tomorrow – if the weather is nice."

4 **inside** [ɪn'saɪd] hinein • 12 **tongue** [tʌŋ] Zunge • 17 **a lot of** [ə 'lɒt əv] viel • 27 **to feel** [fi:l] fühlen • 28 **enemy** ['enəmi] Feind/-in • 32 **tomorrow** [tə'mɒrəʊ] morgen • **if** [ɪf] wenn, falls

This is a funny plan. Why does Pharos talk about the weather? Then he says, "There are so many tourists outside the Palace it's easy to get you in through the back door."

Well, I do not really think that it is easy, but Pharos knows better. And yes, what we read about him in the newspaper later is a terrible story. But wait … I think I am going too fast with my story.

3 Two rats

"Hey, Ratty, did you hear this? We must tell the boss what the three of them said. I think we've got a problem now. Pharos knows too much, and Sir Fox is clever … too clever! I think we must take more spoons tonight, or our rat brother cannot be free."

"Hey, Roddy, not so fast – what do you mean?"

"Well, Ratty, you know the boss is terrible. He wants the spoons or he says our brother must die! He wants the spoons so much. He saw them when he repaired the Queen's cupboard."

"Oh no, our poor brother – so we must do what the boss says. Let's go and tell him about Pharos."

4 How they find out more

"We must find out more about Pharos," Dr Catson says, "we must also find out why there are so many tourists outside Buckingham Palace if the weather is nice. Can we really trust him?"

My assistant likes books, so he goes to the library. There he can read books and look up things on the Internet. First he reads an interesting website about corgis.

---

9 **did you hear** [ˌdɪd jə ˈhɪə] hast du gehört • 16 **to die** [daɪ] sterben • 17 **saw** [sɔː] sah • **repaired** [rɪˈpeəd] reparierte • 24 **to trust** [trʌst] trauen

Find out about Pharos's family name on the website on this page.

In this part of the story, there are some clues. Try and find them, but do not try to understand every English word. There is a lot of information, but if you are clever like Sir Fox and Dr Catson, you can find what you need.

The Welsh Corgi

The Welsh Corgi is a dog from Wales. Corgi means "dwarf dog" in Welsh. A dwarf is a very small person or animal. Their job was to herd sheep. Corgis are very intelligent and are very good friends.

There are two kinds of Welsh Corgis: the Cardigan and the Pembroke. The Cardigan is bigger, with round ears and a tail like a fox. The Pembroke has got smaller ears. Pembrokes have got a very short tail. They can be black, brown and white. The Pembroke was made popular by Queen Elizabeth II, they are her favourite dogs.

The Cardigan Corgi's tail is long.

The Pembroke Corgi's tail is very short and its ears are smaller.

8 **Welsh** [welʃ] walisisch • 10 **dwarf** [dwɔ:f] Zwerg • 11 **was** [wɒz] war • **to herd** [hɜ:d] hüten, bewachen • 15 **Cardigan** ['kɑ:dɪgən] *Hunderasse* • 24 **was made popular** [wəz ˌmeɪd 'pɒpjələ] wurde bekannt

Then he reads a tourist guide book.

Have a look at the tourist guide book. Why are there so many tourists outside the Palace? There are important clues on this page! Think of the weather, the day and the time.

Changing of the Guard Ceremony at Buckingham Palace

From August to about April the Guard Ceremony takes place every other day, Monday, Wednesday, Friday, Sunday, Tuesday, Thursday, Saturday and then Monday again. From April to July it takes place every day.
The ceremony starts at 11.30 am. Get to Buckingham Palace early for a good position. But you do not have to stand in front of Buckingham Palace to get the best view of the ceremony.
The nearest Underground stations are Victoria Station and Green Park. You can also go to the Palace from St. James's Park.

IN VERY WET WEATHER AND RAIN THE CHANGING OF THE GUARD AT BUCKINGHAM PALACE WILL NOT TAKE PLACE.

6 **Changing of the Guard** [ˌtʃeɪndʒɪŋ əv ðə 'gɑ:d] Wachablösung • **ceremony** ['serɪməni] Zeremonie • 8 **early** ['ɜ:li] früh • **position** [pə'zɪʃn] Position • 9 **to take place** [teɪk 'pleɪs] stattfinden • 11 **view** [vju:] Sicht

STOP What can Sir Fox and Dr Catson do now?
Can they trust Pharos?

"So, what do you think about Pharos, my dear Catson?" I ask him later. "Can we trust him? And can we really get into Buckingham Palace or not? And can we find the thief?"

"Oh, Sir Fox, there are many stories about Buckingham Palace. Do you know that there's a police station at the Palace? Of course, security at the Palace is high, but it's not perfect. For example, in 1981 some German tourists climbed into the gardens of the Palace and camped there. And one morning there was a man on the Queen's bed! And when Queen Victoria lived in the Palace, a 12-year-old boy lived in the Palace for a year!"

"Yes, well, you clever cat, let's see what happens. We can go to the Palace tomorrow if the weather is nice and talk to Pharos. Of course I don't want to live there for a year! I think that when we're inside, your good eyes and my perfect nose can help us to catch the thief really fast."

5 Shock

"Sir Fox, Sir Fox, look at this!" It is 7 o'clock in the morning. Dr Catson runs into my room.

"What is it, Dr Catson? You look like … oh, I don't know."

"Well, it's terrible … you know … Pharos …" He shows me the newspaper. This is what it says:

8 police station [pəˈliːs ˌsteɪʃn] Polizeirevier • **9 security** [sɪˈkjʊərəti] Sicherheitsvorkehrungen • **high** [haɪ] hoch • **11 climbed** [klaɪmd] kletterten • **camped** [kæmpt] zelteten, kampierten • **13 lived** [lɪvd] lebte

There is again an important clue!

The Daily Mare

10th December

Princess Anne's dog kills Queen's corgi

One of the Queen's corgis dies after an attack by one of Princess Anne's bull terriers.

On Monday Princess Anne was at Buckingham Palace. The corgis ran out to say hello to her. Then Princess Anne's bull terrier bit the corgi.

Best friend

The Queen and her daughter are very shocked by the death of the Queen's corgi. The dog was Pharos, one of her best friends.

There is no news from Buckingham Palace yet. The Queen and her daughter tried to help the corgi. But Pharos died in the arms of the Queen. Princess Anne says, "I don't understand. My dog is a good dog."

So Pharos is dead. Now the story is really terrible – and we must find out more. But how can we get inside?

Go back to the map on pages 30 and 31and find out how Dr Catson and Sir Fox can get to Buckingham Palace.

It is hard to get to the Palace. It is OK for a cat like my partner, but people do not like foxes in London. I am OK because I know how to get from A to B in the city.

Now we are in the Palace. I am happy, but I am also very tired. I hear a lot of people, and I smell a lot of tourists, too. Terrible!

2 **The Daily Mare** [ðə ˌdeɪli ˈmeə] *Name einer Zeitung* • 10 **ran** [ræn] rannten • 12 **bit** [bɪt] biss • 13 **yet** [jet] noch … nicht • 14 **tried** [traɪd] versuchten • 16 **death** [deθ] Tod

6 At the Palace

At the Palace, one of the Queen's younger corgis is waiting for us. He looks very sad. And he looks nervous, too.

"Good morning, gentlemen. I know about you. Pharos ... well, he told us everything, and now he's dead." The dog cannot go on. We understand. He thinks that he is in danger, too, and that someone can kill him, too.

I can smell danger now. After some time, the corgi tells us the new plan: There is a sad party for Pharos in the Palace. When the food comes, we can sit under a big pot. We must wait in the kitchen until evening. A lady helps in the kitchen and she has got very bad eyes. For her, we are just a cat and one of the dogs.

"But I'm a fox, not a corgi," I protest. The dog and Dr Catson just look at me. "Come on, Sir Fox, do you want to get into the Palace or not?"

So we wait in the garden until evening. We look at all the things in our bags. "We can't take all of this into the Palace! Let's see what we really need." Dr Catson says.

STOP Which things do you think are useful for their job? If you need help with the words, check page 24.

4 **told** [təʊld] erzählte • 9 **pot** [pɒt] Topf • 10 **until** [ʌn'tɪl] bis

"Hey, you, come on. The food is here now, so you can come in!" the corgi says. Dr Catson and I are sleeping, but a cat and a fox have got very good ears. So we hear the voice. It is the nervous corgi. "Come on, quick." He looks so young ... and so nervous. I can smell that he is nervous. He shows us the way to the kitchen. We must be very careful in the Palace because of all the cameras.

"Here's some food for you. You have 30 minutes to eat, and then I will take you to the State Dining Room."

Dr Catson and I have an excellent meal in the Palace. The food – fruit, sandwiches, pudding and cheese – is very good. I like the white wine.

Then we ask the nervous corgi some questions about the room. Now my assistant is nervous. "Do you think I will see the Queen?" he asks five times in ten minutes!

"Well, I don't know, but I think we will see a thief tonight!"

7 Two rats again

"Ouch – not so fast."

"Oh, come on, Ratty, it's time to go."

"No, Roddy, I don't want to go back into that dark tunnel."

"Well, I don't like the tunnel, but we must get more spoons. And you know what will happen to our rat brother ... If we don't get the spoons, he must die. You know I can't go alone. You know that!"

"Is this the last night tonight?"

"I don't think so ... there are some more spoons, and the boss wants them all. Just think of your brother! And don't forget the corgi ... do you want to end like him? You know the boss's bull terrier. His bull terrier is a friend of Princess Anne's dog. And the boss trains Princess Anne's dogs. A bull terrier has terrible teeth."

7 **careful** ['keəfʊl] vorsichtig • 20 **dark** [dɑ:k] dunkel • 32 **teeth** [ti:θ] Zähne

"OK, OK … but what does the boss's letter say? Where can we give him the spoons this time?"

"No problem, you can read the letter later, it's all here in my bag. Now, let's go!"

8 At night

We are in the State Dining Room now … under the table. It is dark, very dark. But a fox can see at night. There is only one door into the room, and two windows. We can see the cupboard. It is very, very old, and very, very beautiful. It is big, too. The Queen has got one key to open the cupboard, and her key is always with her.

Which is the right key?

The Queen's dog tells us that there are eleven spoons missing already. So the thief has eleven spoons. But how? The thief must come at night … Tonight we must stop the thief.

The night is very long, and it is very quiet. Dr Catson looks at the door, and I look at the cupboard. But there is no thief. Outside, we can hear Big Ben … one o'clock, two o'clock, three o'clock. No thief.

I know that thieves come in the night when everyone is in bed, so we wait and wait. Four o'clock. I can hear everything in the Palace: A clock goes tick-tock, someone opens a window. I hear a spoon in a cup of tea. I can smell everything: Food from the kitchen, old shoes, people. But there is no thief.

Suddenly, I hear a sound. From the cupboard! Dr Catson looks at me. Somebody is **in** the cupboard. But we cannot see anything, and we cannot open the cupboard. So we wait and wait. Can the thief open the cupboard from the inside? We can stop him when he comes out of the cupboard. But there is no thief. The door of the cupboard does not open, and the noise in the cupboard goes away. We wait and wait, but the noise does not come back. It is seven thirty and people are getting up. Then the Queen gets up. At eight thirty the Queen has her breakfast.

9 The clue

"Dr Catson, wake up!"

"What is it? – Oh, wow, there she is."

The Queen comes into the room. She carefully closes the door. We are alone in the room with Her Majesty, but she cannot see us. We are under a table. She walks over to the cupboard. I can smell her nice perfume. And we can see her legs and her slippers.

2 **somebody** ['sʌmbədi] jemand • 3 **anything** ['eniθɪŋ] nichts • 11 **Wake up!** [weɪk 'ʌp] Wach auf! • 14 **Her Majesty** [hɜː 'mædʒəsti] Ihre königliche Hoheit • 17 **slippers** ['slɪpəz] Hausschuhe

She checks the door again. Now she takes out a key and opens the cupboard. I am very nervous now. We cannot look into the cupboard, but the Queen takes out a box and comes over to the table. She sits down and starts counting her spoons. "One, two, three ..."

Dr Catson and I know that there are not enough spoons in the cupboard. We look at the open cupboard. And this is when we see the small hole in the back of the cupboard. And there is something white in the cupboard, too. We can see it in the mirror inside the cupboard from where we are. It is paper, and it is dirty. The thief must have lost it!

The thief has lost a letter in the cupboard.
Dr Catson and Sir Fox can see it in the mirror of the cupboard. What does it say?

1 to check [tʃek] überprüfen • **6 enough** [ɪ'nʌf] genug • **8 hole** [həʊl] Loch • **10 mirror** ['mɪrə] Spiegel • **11 have lost** [hæv 'lɒst] verloren haben

There is a shriek from the Queen. "Thirty-nine," she says. "Just thirty-nine." She puts the box back in the cupboard, locks the door and leaves the room. She looks very, very sad.

"Come on, Catson. Quick! We must go to the London Eye and catch the thief there!"

"But how do we know who he is? And how can we get on the flight? A fox and a cat can't get into the capsules!"

10 At the London Eye

The corgis help us to get out of the Palace. They are shocked when they hear about our night in the State Dining Room, about the thief, the Queen and the note. Now we have got one hour to get from the Palace to the London Eye, but it is hard. We must get through St. James's Park. We must walk past the Houses of Parliament and Westminster Abbey. Then we must cross the River Thames. People in London walk very fast, so they do not see us. The tourists look at the sights and they look through the lenses of their cameras, but they do not look at small animals.

At ten o'clock we are at the London Eye. We are lucky; there are a lot of people there. They are buying their tickets and are waiting for their flight and their capsule. Dr Catson and I sit in a bush and look at the people. There are many children from Africa, from Asia, and from America. People speak English, Chinese, Japanese and French. But we cannot see a brown bag.

At ten-thirty, 20 people go into the capsule. They go in one by one. The door of the capsule closes and the flight begins. Because the flight is 30 minutes, we now have got 30 minutes to think and to make plans.

---

1 **shriek** [ʃri:k] Schrei • 3 **to lock** [lɒk] verschließen • 8 **flight** [flaɪt] *hier:* Fahrt • **capsule** ['kæpsju:l] *hier:* Kapsel des Riesenrades • 17 **lens** [lenz] Linse

Find the rats in the picture.

There are more clues in the picture. Who is the thief, and why?

"Hey, that's brilliant, Sir Fox!" Dr Catson says a few minutes later. "You're wonderful!"

11 Arrest

When a man comes out of the capsule, we see his small brown bag. But we cannot see the rats. So we follow the man. He does not go to the Palace because there is no ceremony today. In December, the Changing of the Guard Ceremony is not every day. He walks for about 20 minutes, then he stops in front of a shop. He takes out a key and opens the shop door. The name of the shop is

ARTHUR S. TEALER, ANTIQUES.

He looks very happy. He goes into the shop and closes the door. CLOSED, it says on the door. "I think we know enough," I tell Dr Catson. We go back to my office and phone Foxland Yard. We tell them to take a look at the antiques in Mr Tealer's shop.

In the afternoon, we switch on the radio. This is what we hear:

arrest [ə'rest] Festnahme • **2 to follow** ['fɒləʊ] folgen • **8 antiques** [æn'ti:ks] Antiquitäten • **10 closed** [kləʊzd] geschlossen • **14 to switch on** [swɪtʃ 'ɒn] einschalten

“Well,” I tell Dr Catson, “but we do!”

“Poor Pharos and poor Princess Anne – they have nothing to do with the thief. But Mr Tealer’s bull terrier asked Princess Anne’s dog to kill Pharos. And all the rats just worked for him to help their brothers!” Dr Catson says.

“Sir Fox, how do you do it? You’re a wonderful detective – the best detective in the world.”

4 **asked** [ɑ:skt] bat • 5 **worked** [wɜ:kt] arbeiteten

Fun exercises for "Sir Fox Bones"

1 Words and pictures

Look up the words in your dictionary and match them with the pictures.

sunglasses

torch

magnifying glasses

scarf

sleeping bag

bars of chocolate

gloves

alarm clock

2 Crazy text

Find the correct order.

1. A bull terrier kills Pharos.
2. A rat is listening when Sir Fox, Dr Catson and Pharos are talking.
3. Dr Catson is in the library.
4. Sir Fox and Dr Catson wait in the kitchen.
5. The rats are in the capsule.
6. Pharos is at Sir Fox's office.
7. Sir Fox and Dr Catson follow the antique dealer.

3 A quiz

Match the words with the ideas from the text.
Then ask questions. Your partner must answer them.

Who … | Where … | When … | Why … | What …

… takes the spoons from the cupboard?
… in December can you go and see the 'Changing of the Guard'?
… is there a 'sad party' for Pharos?
… do they go to the London Eye?
… does Mr Tealer work?
… cannot go on the London Eye?
… does the Quuen do after breakfast?

Find more questions and answers and make a quiz.

4 Dr Catson's diary

In the evening Dr Catson writes in his diary.
He is very tired and so he makes mistakes.

Can you find them?

4th July

Wow! This day is funny! Sir Fox and I went to Buckingham Palace to help the Queen. She wants her rings back. We wait and wait in the State Dining Room but the thief did not come. At 9 o'clock in the morning we hear something inside the cupboard. But we cannot see anything. Then the Queen comes and opens the cupboard. She sees that the thief has got more of her rings now. She is happy. In the cupboard there is a paper from the thief. The Queen reads it and asks us to catch him at the London Ear. We tell Foxland Yard and they arrest the thief.

---

went [went] gingen

5 A picture story

Draw one scene of the book. Collect the pictures in class. Now try to find out what comes first, what happens next etc. Tell the story in your own words.

6 On the phone

Sir Fox calls Foxland Yard to tell them about Mr Tealer. What does he say?

Make a dialogue.

INSPECTOR Y: Hello, your password, please!
SIR FOX: S-E-N-O-B
INSPECTOR Y: Oh, hello, Sir Fox Bones.
SIR FOX: Hello there, please give me Inspector X … Hello, I must tell you something very important …

7 A thank-you note

Ratty and Roddy write a thank-you note to Sir Fox. What do they write? How is their brother?

Write the thank-you note.

8 A 'mini' project

Find out more about:

- Scotland Yard
- Sherlock Holmes
- The London Eye
- Buckingham Palace
- The Queen

You can find information in books or on the Internet.

Solutions

Before you read

1 The cover

a) –

b)

M	D	N	G	J	I	E	W	Q	F
Q	U	E	E	N	J	D	X	D	W
W	Q	B	T	H	B	E	T	I	C
D	O	N	F	E	U	A	F	S	R
G	P	A	L	A	C	E	O	U	G
K	H	U	V	P	K	T	S	B	E
W	A	I	F	H	I	G	I	S	A
D	S	P	O	X	N	H	Z	V	Y
B	H	X	X	B	G	O	Z	G	E
M	E	H	O	C	H	R	E	Y	D
W	Q	H	U	S	A	A	N	M	K
A	X	S	I	I	M	T	E	N	L

2 Detectives

a) –

b) –

solution [səˈluːʃn] Lösung

Fun exercises for "Sir Fox Bones"

1 Words and pictures

sunglasses (Sonnenbrille), torch (Taschenlampe), magnifying glasses (Lupe), scarf (Schal), sleeping bag (Schlafsack), bars of chocolate (Schokoladenriegel), gloves (Handschuhe), alarm clock (Wecker)

2 Crazy text

6., 2., 3., 1., 4., 5., 7

3 A quiz

Who takes the spoons from the cupboard? – The rats take the spoons.

When in December can you go and see the 'Changing of the Guard'? – You can go and see it every other day.

Why is there a 'sad party' for Pharos? – Because he is dead.

Why do they go to the London Eye? – They want to catch the thief there.

Where does Mr Tealer work? – He works in a shop.

Who cannot go on the London Eye? – The rats cannot go on the London Eye.

What does the Queen do after breakfast? – She counts her spoons.

4 Dr Catson's diary

4th December

Wow! This day is funny! Sir Fox and I went to Buckingham Palace to help the Queen. She wants her spoons back. We wait and wait in the State Dining Room but the thief did not come. At 4 o'clock in the morning we hear something inside the cupboard. But we cannot see anything. Then the Queen comes and opens the cupboard. She sees that the thief has got more of her spoons. She is sad. In the cupboard there is a paper from the thief. We can read it in the mirror of the cupboard door. We now know that the thief is at the London Eye. We go there and find out who the thief is. We tell Foxland Yard and they arrest the thief.

5 A picture story –

6 On the phone

INSPECTOR Y: Hello, your password, please!
SIR FOX: S-E-N-O-B
INSPECTOR Y: Oh, hello, Sir Fox Bones.
SIR FOX: Hello there, please give me Inspector X … Hello, I must tell you something very important …
INSPECTOR X: Yes, you can speak. The line is safe.
SIR FOX: Do you know Mr Arthur Tealer's Antiques?
INSPECTOR X: Yes, Mr Tealer trains bull terriers.
SIR FOX: Yes, and he also has got the Queen's spoons from Buckingham Palace. My partner and I know that rats work for him and take the spoons out of the Palace. You must arrest him now!
INSPECTOR X: Yes, of course. Thank you for the information Sir Fox.

7 A thank-you note

Hello Sir Fox,
Thank you very much! Our brother is free again. He's OK and we are so happy that we don't have to take spoons from the Palace and don't have to go back in the dark tunnel.
Yours, Ratty and Roddy

8 A 'mini' project –

LONDON
Swiss Cottage
Belsize Road
CAMDEN
Camden Market
Regent's Park
Outer Circle
Albany Street
Hampstead Road
Maida Vale
Park Road
SIR FOX BONES
Madame Tussaud's
Butcher Road
Gloucester Place
Marylebone Road
Westway A40
Edgeware Road
Wigmore Street
Oxford Street
Oxford Circus
Regent St
Bond Street
Marble Arch
Notting Hill Carnival
NOTTING HILL
Bayswater Road
Hyde Park
The Serpentine
Rotten Row
Piccadilly
Green Park
Kensington Road
Buckingham Palace
National History Museum
Brompton Road
Sloane Street
Heathrow Airport
Cromwell Road
Victoria Station
Brompton Road
Fulham Road
King's Road
Wimbledon
Richmond
Chelsea Embankment

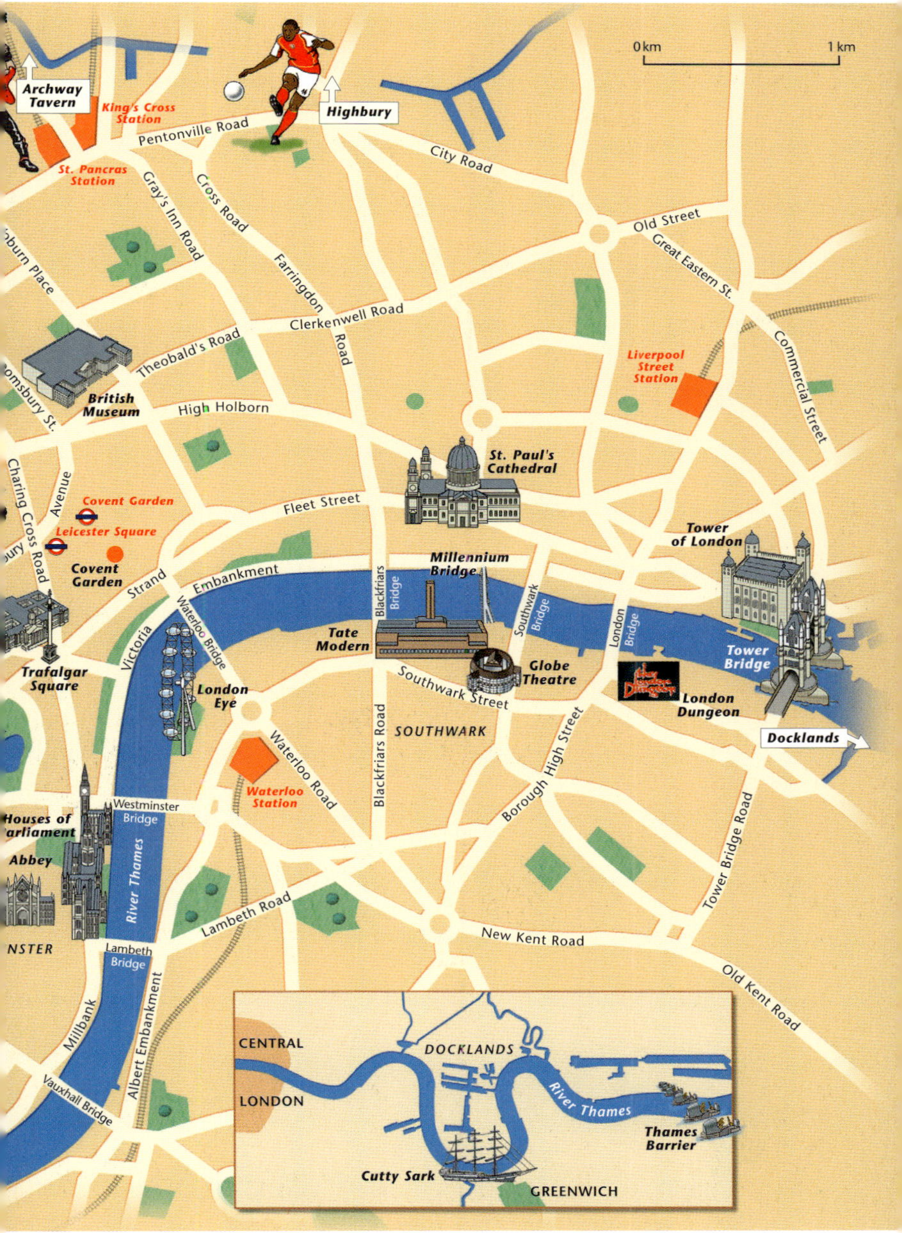

0 km
1 km
Archway Tavern
Highbury
King's Cross Station
St. Pancras Station
Pentonville Road
City Road
Gray's Inn Road
Cross Road
Old Street
Great Eastern St.
Farringdon Road
Clerkenwell Road
Theobald's Road
Commercial Street
Liverpool Street Station
British Museum
High Holborn
St. Paul's Cathedral
Charing Cross Road
Avenue
Covent Garden
Leicester Square
Fleet Street
Tower of London
Covent Garden
Millennium Bridge
Strand
Embankment
Blackfriars Bridge
Southwark Bridge
London Bridge
Waterloo Bridge
Tate Modern
Globe Theatre
Tower Bridge
Victoria
Trafalgar Square
London Eye
Southwark Street
London Dungeon
Docklands
SOUTHWARK
Blackfriars Road
Borough High Street
Waterloo Road
Waterloo Station
Westminster Bridge
Houses of Parliament
Abbey
River Thames
Tower Bridge Road
Lambeth Road
New Kent Road
Lambeth Bridge
Old Kent Road
Millbank
Albert Embankment
Vauxhall Bridge
CENTRAL LONDON
DOCKLANDS
River Thames
Thames Barrier
Cutty Sark
GREENWICH

Bildquellen:
S. 11: (1) Mauritius (Gerard Lacz), Mittenwald; (2) stocktogo.com (RF/Jeffrey Ong Guo Xiong), New York, NY; S. 12: Corel Corporation, Unterschleissheim; S. 14: Corel Corporation, Unterschleissheim; S. 26: Fotosearch RF (PhotoDisc), Waukesha, WI